THE DRAWINGS OF REMBRANDT

itish Museum

Museum

m

reet, London w.1
Road, London n.w.1
r & Co. Ltd,
ndon w.c.1
Office,
ay,

7

EM)

N

Limited
ers
ess

A NEGRO COMMANDER AND KETTLE DRUMMER
*c. 1638. Pen and ink with brown wash, red chalk
and yellow water-colour, heightened
with white. 22.9 × 17 cm*

© 1962 The Trustees of the Br

PUBLISHED BY
The Trustees of the British
AND SOLD AT
The British Museu
AND BY
Bernard Quaritch Ltd, 11 Grafton St
Cambridge University Press, 200 Eusto
Kegan, Paul, Trench Trubne
43 Great Russell Street, Lo
Her Majesty's Stationery
York House, Kingsw
London W.C.2

*Printed by
Eyre and Spottiswoode
Her Majesty's Prin
at The Chiswick P
London*

LIST OF ILLUSTRATIONS

	Star of the Kings	*cover*
	A Negro commander and kettle drummer	*frontispiece*
1	The Entombment of Christ (originally the Raising of Lazarus)	*page* 33
2	Christ walking on the waves (*c.* 1633)	34
3	The Good Samaritan arriving at the inn	35
4	Jacob and Rachel listening to an account of Joseph's dreams (?)	36
5	Esau selling his birthright to Jacob	36
6	David and Absalom	37
7	Christ walking on the waves (*c.* 1659)	38
8	A scene from the life of Pyrrhus	39
9	Copy after Mantegna's 'Calumny of Apelles'	40
10	Copy after Leonardo's 'Last Supper'	41
11	Copy after a Mogul miniature (Four Dervishes)	41
12	Self-portrait	42
13	Cornelis Claesz Anslo	42
14	Jan Cornelis Sylvius	43
15	A lady holding a fan	43
16	A woman in bed (Saskia?)	44
17	Studies of a beggar walking on crutches	44
18	Two women teaching a child to walk	45
19	A child being taught to walk	45

20	A girl sleeping (Hendrickje Stoffels?)	*page* 46
21	A young man asleep (Titus?)	47
22	A girl seated (Hendrickje Stoffels?)	47
23	Diana at the bath	48
24	The artist drawing from a model	49
25	Seated female nude	49
26	An elephant	50
27	The Amstel river near Kostverloren	51
28	A chained lioness	51
29	House amidst trees	52

LIFE OF

REMBRANDT

1606	Born on 15th July at Leiden, the son of a miller.
1620	Enrolled as a student at Leiden University.
1621	Apprenticed to Jacob van Swanenburgh, a minor architectural painter in Leiden, with whom he spent three years.
1624/5	Worked for six months as a pupil of Pieter Lastman in Amsterdam.
c. 1625	Set up as an independent painter in Leiden, possibly sharing a studio with Jan Lievens.
1631	Moved to Amsterdam, where he lived in a house in St Anthonie Breerstraat, belonging to Hendrick van Ulenborch, an art dealer and painter.
1632	Painted *The Anatomy Lesson of Dr Tulp*.
1634	Married Saskia van Ulenborch, daughter of the late burgomaster of Leeuwarden, and a cousin of Hendrick van Ulenborch.
1639	Purchased a house in St Anthonie Breerstraat, Amsterdam (now a Museum known as the Rembrandthuis).
1640	Death of his mother.
1641	Birth of his son, Titus, the only surviving child by Saskia.
1642	Death of Saskia. Painted the so-called *Night Watch*.
c. 1645	Hendrickje Stoffels entered Rembrandt's home as a servant.
1654	Birth of his daughter, Cornelia, by Hendrickje Stoffels.
1656	To avoid bankruptcy Rembrandt's property was liquidated. An inventory of his possessions was drawn up, and describes his extensive collection of works of art.

1660	His son Titus and Hendrickje Stoffels formed a business partnership and made Rembrandt their employee, in order to protect him from his creditors.
1661	Painted *The Conspiracy of Claudius Civilis* for the newly built Town Hall in Amsterdam, but did not meet with approval. It was removed soon after, and replaced by a work of one of his pupils.
1662	Painted *The Syndics*.
c. 1662	Death of Hendrickje Stoffels.
1668	Death of his son Titus.
1669	Died on 4th October and was buried in the Westerkerk in Amsterdam.

N O T E

All drawings in the British Museum mentioned in the text are given with their relevant number in Hind's catalogue (see SELECTED LITERATURE, *pp. 28-9) e.g., H.82; in the case of drawings in other collections, reference is made to Benesch's catalogue, e.g., B.654.*

THE DRAWINGS OF
REMBRANDT

THE BRITISH MUSEUM possesses just over a hundred generally accepted drawings by Rembrandt. Though this amounts to under one tenth of his total output, the collection is one of the most representative, particularly when his drawings are considered in conjunction with his etchings, of which the Museum has possibly the finest collection in existence. The drawings in the Museum cover every category of his work and include a number of masterpieces; only the landscapes fall below the high standard set by the other drawings. The most important sources of the Museum's collection are the Payne Knight bequest of 1824, the Malcolm collection, purchased in 1895, and the Salting bequest of 1910; these account for about three-quarters of the total number, the remainder being made up of individual purchases and bequests.

The drawings by Rembrandt in the Museum were catalogued in 1915 by A. M. Hind, though since then the collection has been enriched by a number of important acquisitions. Hind arranged the drawings according to his estimate of their chronological order, with the exception of the landscapes which he placed in a group at the end. Since the appearance of the catalogue some forty-five years ago, extensive research has increased our knowledge of the subject, particularly with regard to the dating of drawings; even so, this still remains a matter of discussion, and personal opinions often differ considerably. A general stylistic analysis of Rembrandt's development as a draughtsman is, therefore, very difficult. Only when the purpose of the drawing has been taken into consideration does the trend of his stylistic development as a draughtsman become clear. The standard of finish in a painting or an etching, which makes the comparison of one work with another permissible, does not apply to his drawings, which may vary from a few lines in pen and ink to an elaborate study in a combination of techniques.

Study of Rembrandt's drawings also raises a problem of connoisseurship. The Rembrandtesque style is easy to recognize, but in some cases, relatively few in comparison with the large number of undoubtedly authentic drawings, it is hard to make the final decision whether the drawing is by the master or not. Some of these doubtful drawings are copies made by pupils or later artists after originals by Rembrandt.

From c. 1628 onwards, and throughout the remainder of his life, Rembrandt had a succession of pupils whom, as we know from the writings of one of them, Samuel van Hoogstraeten, he encouraged to copy the drawings of other artists; and the large number of existing copies after Rembrandt's own drawings show to what extent his advice was followed. Where original and copy both exist the difference can quite easily be detected, e.g. *Esau selling his birthright to Jacob*, (H. 129), *The miraculous draught of fishes* (H. 130), *The flight into Egypt* (H. 131), *An artist painting the portrait of a young woman* (H. 132), and *A reclining lion* (H. 133), all of which are copies after known original drawings, the last after a drawing in the British Museum (H. 44). In every case both original and copy are almost identical in detail, but when compared, the hesitancy and lack of vigour of the copy is readily discernible. When, however, the original no longer exists, a copy can often give rise to confusion. *The sacrifice of Iphigenia* (H. 92) was accepted as an original by Hind, but a cut down version of the same composition which has come to light at Besançon (B. 979), has shown the British Museum drawing to be only a copy. Copyists were particularly skilful in reproducing every detail and flourish of the pen; and, therefore, in trying to determine the authenticity of a doubtful drawing, one often has to rely on the subjective criterion of quality.

Another confusing category is composed of original drawings by pupils or followers, e.g. Govaert Flinck or Philips Koninck, who on occasions came deceptively close to Rembrandt's manner. *A Woman seated* (H. 29) is a case in point; its high quality has never been in doubt, and some critics accept it as an original by Rembrandt, whilst others think the style not close enough to that of Rembrandt himself, and that it is the work of a gifted pupil.

With an artist of Rembrandt's versatility we can never be certain of immediately identifying his hand in every mood. A drawing, which appears at first glance uncharacteristic, may on closer acquaintance reveal itself as an authentic work, but done in an unusual moment. It is, perhaps, a measure of his greatness that there can never be a definitive catalogue of his drawings.

Rembrandt's technique was relatively simple. He nearly always drew on small sheets of white paper, though he occasionally used a large sheet in his earlier work. The predominant medium throughout his life was pen and ink. He employed black and red chalk, a considerable amount in the first half of his life, but very rarely after the end of the 1640's. The pen drawings are for the most part in brown ink, though black ink, sometimes mixed with brown, is also found. As a young man he drew more often with a quill pen, which has greater flexibility and allows easier elaboration of detail than the reed pen, to which he turned more and more in later years, and whose soft, broad line, similar to that of a brush, did justice to the simplified, more monumental style of his last works. The brush was frequently used for laying in washes, and occasionally for drawing the outline as well, as, for example, in the famous drawing of *A girl sleeping* (Hendrickje Stoffels?) (H. 97) (FIG. 20). White body-colour was employed, sometimes for heightening, but more often for cancelling unsatisfactory parts of a drawing. Examples of both uses can be seen in *Cornelis Claesz Anslo* (H. 59) (FIG. 13); the height of the sitter's hat has been lowered by the addition of white body-colour, while the sense of volume of his body has been increased by the application of the same medium. As a rule the media of pen and chalk do not appear together in the same drawing, but sometimes he employed a combination, e.g. *A negro commander and kettle drummer* (H. 8) (frontispiece), drawn in pen and brown ink with wash, red chalk, yellow water-colour and white body-colour, or the *Lamentation over the dead Christ* (H. 60), drawn in pen and brown ink and red chalk over which the artist has worked in oil paint.

Art historians sometimes tend to concentrate more on enumerating the influences of other works of art on a particular artist than on defining his own contribution. The balance between the two must, of course, vary according to the artist. In Rembrandt's case every external influence was completely absorbed and became the expression of his own personality. Even in his earliest drawings a marked individuality and independence is already apparent. His first master, Jacob van Swanenburgh, appears to have left him untouched. Pieter Lastman with whom he worked very briefly had a certain influence, though the drawings exhibit the differences between the two artists rather than the similarities. Rembrandt's refusal to follow the fashionable practice of going to Italy to complete his training is well known, and at the age of nineteen he set up as an independent artist in Leiden. From then on he followed his own course.

Although Rembrandt's drawings are entirely personal, he did not shut his eyes to the works of other artists; the inventory of his possessions made in 1656 describes his extensive collection of works of art. Furthermore, Samuel van Hoogstraeten, as has been mentioned, describes how Rembrandt recommended his pupils to copy the drawings of older artists. The number of copies he himself made show that in this he was no mere theorist, and his advice reflected his own practice. He made drawn copies after paintings and drawings by such artists as Mantegna, Leonardo, Raphael and his School, Titian and Lastman (his own Italianate master), and these prove that his unwillingness to go to Italy was not due to any lack of interest in Italian art.

About 1635 Rembrandt made three copies after Leonardo's *Last Supper*, which he knew from a Milanese sixteenth-century engraving. The first in Dresden (B. 443) is a fairly literal copy, while the last in Berlin (B. 445) dated 1635, shows an extensive reworking of the composition. Between the two comes the red chalk study of the left-hand part of the composition (H. 3) (FIG. 10), which shows a number of variations from Leonardo's original in the extreme left-hand group. These three copies are a revealing study of Rembrandt's process of thought. In the first drawing he was intent on absorbing Leonardo's composition, in the second he introduced some of his own ideas, whilst the third is an entirely personal solution in the baroque idiom of the early seventeenth century. His interest in *The Last*

Supper was not, however, confined to these three drawings. In a painting three years later, treating an entirely different subject, *Samson's wedding*, dated 1638, in Dresden, he introduced an echo of Leonardo in the way the guests are composed on either side of the central figure of Delilah. Nearly twenty years later the figure of Christ in the etching *Christ at Emmaus* (Hind, *Etchings*, 282), dated 1654, is still reminiscent of Leonardo's Christ.

At a slightly later date Rembrandt became interested in the art of Mantegna, and reflections of his interest can be seen in the etching *The Virgin and Child in the clouds* (Hind, *Etchings*, 186), dated 1641. In the following decade *c*. 1655 he copied Mantegna's drawing of *The Calumny of Apelles*; both original and copy (H. 80) (FIG. 9) are now in the British Museum. Rembrandt followed Mantegna's composition, even down to copying in an Italianate hand the inscriptions which identify the figures in the drama. He followed the artist's technique of hatched lines, but he drew these more broadly, and the result, which suggests tone rather than the sculptural quality of the original, is a totally personal interpretation that could only have come from the hand of Rembrandt. In contrast, Rubens' copies after Mantegna show a scrupulous regard for reproducing the exact character of the original.

Rembrandt's taste was not confined exclusively to European art, and, in fact, the copies he made after a series of Mogul miniatures are the most numerous of his studies after other works of art. In 1747 Jonathan Richardson the elder possessed twenty-five of these copies by Rembrandt; only nineteen exist today, and six of these are in the British Museum (H. 74-79). In the eighteenth century a series of Mogul miniatures, some of which are similar in composition to several of Rembrandt's copies, were incorporated into the decorative scheme of one of the rooms at Schloss Schönbrunn, Vienna, where they can be seen today. Whether they were Rembrandt's direct models, as has often been said, is open to doubt. There is a certain amount of evidence that the Schönbrunn miniatures came from Constantinople and not Holland, and in any case may well have been made at a later date than Rembrandt's copies. A composition in Indian art is often repeated exactly as much as a century later, so that both the Schönbrunn miniatures and Rembrandt's copies may be based on a common source. It has been suggested that the miniatures Rembrandt copied belonged to him and he drew them in

1656 when he was forced to sell all his possessions; one of the items described in the inventory of his collection is '(a book) of curious miniature drawings'. Rembrandt has given a certain authentic flavour to his copies by the use of Japanese paper, though otherwise he has rendered the elaborately finished, highly coloured originals in pen and ink and brown wash. His interest in these Mogul works was not merely that of a collector, and can be seen in the way he adapted the composition of *Four Dervishes seated beneath a tree* (H. 74) (FIG. 11) to his etching, *Abraham entertaining the angels* (Hind, *Etchings*, 286), dated 1656. Abraham and his guests are squatting on the ground in a semi-circular group, similar to that of the four Dervishes drinking tea and telling their beads. This adaptation of an Oriental subject to a Biblical theme shows how Rembrandt was more concerned with the spirit than the letter in his recreation of authentic atmosphere.

Rembrandt regarded drawing as a medium in its own right. The majority of his drawings cannot be connected with either paintings or etchings. No compositional studies exist for many of his large paintings such as *The Anatomy Lesson of Professor Tulp* in The Hague, and the so-called *Night Watch* in Amsterdam, or for his more elaborate etchings for example '*The Hundred Guilder Print*' (Hind, *Etchings*, 236); and one must assume that these elaborate compositions took shape on the canvas or etching plate. The independence of each medium was not, however, entirely exclusive and sometimes he based a painting or an etching on a drawing: drawings connected with other works of art are very well represented in the British Museum. It is difficult to make any firm generalizations about his working method in these cases, and such is the character of some of these drawings that it is not always possible to distinguish between a drawing made specifically as a study in preparation for another work, and a drawing which was afterwards used incidentally as the basis for an etching or painting. Two drawings in the British Museum show careful preparation for etching: *Diana at the bath* (H. 9) (FIG. 23) and (Hind, *Etchings*, 42), c. 1631, and the portrait *Cornelis Claesz Anslo* (H. 59) (FIG. 13), signed and dated 1640, which was etched the following year (Hind, *Etchings*, 187). Both these working drawings are in chalk and the outlines were indented through the paper with a stylus by the artist so that the design was transferred on to the prepared ground of the etching plate. Another example of this type of study is *The artist drawing from a model* (H. 69) (FIG. 24), drawn in pen and ink with the addition of brown wash to depict a strong light cast on the model against the deep shadow of the background; in this case the artist was more concerned with chiaroscuro than outline in his preparatory drawing. The etching (Hind, *Etchings*, 231), in the past considered to be of *c.* 1648 but more probably *c.* 1639, was never finished, and it shows how Rembrandt, when working up a detailed etching, sketched the outlines on the plates with the etching needle with as much freedom as if he were using a pen. He did not follow his drawing line for line but redrew the figures on the plate with numerous alterations. On the other hand, the posthumously etched portrait, *Jan Cornelis Sylvius* (Hind, *Etchings*, 225), dated 1646 was preceded by three drawings (B. 762, 762a and H. 65) devoted to fixing the pose of the sitter. The study in the British Museum (H. 65) (FIG. 14), drawn in vigorous broad pen strokes, is the closest to the etching and probably immediately preceded it.

Only at the beginning of his career, before Rembrandt had acquired fluency in the medium of etching, did he show any dependence on a preparatory drawing, but even then, it was the exception rather than the rule. For Rembrandt drawing and etching were two different means of expression, and he did not consider the one the servant of the other.

The same lack of any regular system of working can be found in the few drawings connected with paintings. *A lady holding a fan* (H. 56) (FIG. 15) is the preparatory study for the painting in Amsterdam, dated 1639. In technique and character it is similar to the drawing of *The artist drawing from a model*, just referred to; pose and disposition of lighting are clearly worked out and are followed closely in the final version. A far more unusual example in Rembrandt's *œuvre* is the drawing *Lamentation over the dead Christ* (H. 60), which belongs more to the Renaissance tradition than Rembrandt's usual practice. This sheet is made up of a number of pieces of paper, each addition acting as a means of correcting unsatisfactory parts of the composition. The figures were drawn in pen and ink and the background details in red chalk, and then Rembrandt elaborated the sheet further by the addition of oil paint. The final version in the National Gallery shows further changes, but still has more the character of an oil sketch than a finished painting.

The examples discussed above show the design fixed in his preparatory study. An early drawing in the Museum, where the artist developed his design in the painting, shows that this method was not invariable. The drawing *Abraham's sacrifice of Isaac* (H. 6) displays his characteristic treatment of composition about 1628/9 when he arranged his figures in a closed sculptural group; the figure of the angel appears dramatically from behind Abraham and gives a suggestion of spiral movement to the group. In the painting in Leningrad, dated 1635, Rembrandt placed the angel at the top left-hand corner, which has the effect of spreading the composition across the canvas and giving the arrangement of the figures a more two-dimensional pattern.

One of the largest groups of Rembrandt drawings are the genre studies made from everyday life with no ulterior purpose in mind. Under this heading it is convenient to discuss figure studies made from a model, as the distinction between the two groups is often hard to sustain. Sketching from everyday life is today a well accepted practice, but in and before Rembrandt's time, it was the exception rather than the rule, and he was the first to realize its full potentialities. Drawing from a posed model was a feature of the Italian tradition, but even here Rembrandt nearly always gives his studies an element of genre by suggesting setting and atmosphere. His approach to art was realistic; he considered life and art, not as two separate entities, but one as the basis of the other, and from the beginning he deliberately turned to nature and took inspiration from his surroundings. Though seventeenth-century Dutch art became almost exclusively concerned with portraying the natural world, it nearly always displays a feeling of detached observation. No other artist succeeded in identifying himself with his subject as closely as Rembrandt did. In his works he shows complete empathy with his subject.

Rembrandt's realism comes out very strongly in his drawings. The studies after life form the basic vocabulary of his artistic language which he then moulded to suit the subject in hand. As one would expect, his genre studies were more common in the first half of his career. Later his knowledge was sufficiently wide for him to draw on his memory without constantly referring back to life, but even then he never entirely abandoned the practice.

Three sketches in the British Museum are devoted to the subject of a child being taught to walk. The first two (H. 4, 5) (FIG. 18), in red chalk, were drawn c. 1637 and show the astonishing certainty and simplicity of his drawing even at this date. The fully expressive shorthand catches a particular moment in this intimate domestic scene. The third sheet, (H. 81) (FIG. 19), which must be one of the last drawings he made, c. 1660, is drawn on the back of a piece of paper containing memoranda written by the artist, and shows a similar scene treated with the same snapshot vividness, though, of course, the style of the drawing has changed. The monumental figures are drawn with block-like simplicity. One line does the work of several before. If anything, this later drawing displays greater psychological concentration on the efforts of the child – seen only from the back – to take its first step. On looking through Rembrandt's studies of this kind one is constantly struck by the acute observation of every facet of daily life. He picks out the smallest incidents – a screaming, kicking child, or a small boy feeling in his pocket for money to buy a pancake – incidents, which were hardly noticed, let alone considered worthy of art.

Rembrandt's deep humanity is manifest in all his work. He constantly depicted people of all kinds with sympathy and understanding. In the 1630's he made numerous studies of beggars, for example FIG. 17 (H. 22-24). A similar interest is found in the work of Callot, who, it is suggested, may have influenced Rembrandt. Though this may well have been so in general terms, Rembrandt's drawings and etchings lack the moralizing qualities of the French artist, who was pointing to the misery and poverty of many aspects of seventeenth-century life. Rembrandt's beggars never shock, and are studied as part of the daily scene; they are above all human beings, though unhappy ones. His work always expresses the emotion of the individual rather than an abstract idea.

In many of Rembrandt's works there is an earthiness which was in strong reaction to the current Italianate taste, so typical, for example, of the work of his master, Pieter Lastman, and one of the characteristics of Dutch art in the first years of the seventeenth-century. Joachim von Sandrart, the seventeenth-century German painter and writer, takes Rembrandt to task for ignoring 'our rules of art' such as the theories of anatomy, proportion and perspective. Rembrandt's answer was simple, but at this date still revolutionary; 'one should be guided only by Nature and no other rules'.

His etching of the massive *Naked woman seated on a mound* (Hind,

c

Etchings, 43), *c.* 1631, as unromantic a model as can be found in any art school, is the superb gesture of defiance of contemporary taste by a young man. Throughout his life he retained a preference for the life of the streets. Even during the years of his marriage to Saskia, when he moved in prosperous bourgeois circles and became a successful portrait painter, he appears more interested in painting the rosettes on a sitter's shoes than the smooth, round, well-fed face of the sitter himself. A beggar with his hands out, an old woman selling pancakes, or an elderly Jew gazing into space always appealed to Rembrandt; indeed he went further and often imbued them with a profundity of his own.

No other artist brings the atmosphere and events of contemporary Amsterdam so vividly before our eyes as Rembrandt in his numerous genre studies. A pageant held in February, 1638 by Constantijn Huyghens, Secretary to the Prince of Orange and a friend of the artist, may well have been the occasion when he made the magnificent drawing *A negro commander and kettle drummer* (H. 8) (frontispiece). *A mounted officer* (H. 7) and two other studies (B. 366, 368) were also probably drawn at the same time.

The old custom, which can still be seen today in the south of Holland, of children processing through the streets bearing a star-shaped lantern on the feast of the Epiphany, did not escape Rembrandt's attention. A drawing, *The Star of the Kings* (H. 31) (reproduced on the cover), of *c.* 1641, depicts this very scene; a small boy holds up the star outside a house, and is surrounded by children of all ages, whose varied emotions range from the awe of the babe in arms to the distress of the small child crying on the right, who refuses to be comforted by the sight of the lantern. The brown wash laid over part of the background probably indicates that the event is taking place at night, as it certainly does in the etching of the same event (Hind, *Etchings*, 254), made about ten years later, *c.* 1652.

One may guess that travelling circuses were the source for the animal studies, which, though few in number, are amongst the most attractive of Rembrandt's drawings. *The elephant* (H. 43) (FIG. 26), *c.* 1637 – there are two other studies in the Albertina, Vienna (B. 457, 458) – shows the artist's ability to suggest with black chalk the wrinkled texture of the animal's skin. No doubt these three drawings prompted the idea of including an elephant in the background of the etching, *Adam and Eve* (Hind, *Etchings*, 159), dated

1638. On another occasion, a lioness, depicted in two drawings now in the British Museum (H. 49, 50) (FIG. 28) was probably the inspiration for the lioness seated in the foreground of the allegorical painting *The Concord of State*, dated 1641, in Rotterdam. The numerous studies of lions – five are in the British Museum (H. 44-48) – are sometimes the work of pupils as well as the master himself. One of the British Museum studies (H. 47) may well have been drawn by a pupil and then corrected in broad pen strokes by Rembrandt. The two studies of a pig (H. 41, 42), drawings which entered the British Museum attributed to Titian, undoubtedly inspired the etching of 1643 (Hind, *Etchings*, 204) and cannot have been far from his mind when he drew *The prodigal son among the swine* (H. 40), which belongs to approximately the same date.

It is above all the artist and his family who are the constant *leitmotif* of his work so that we follow all the events and emotions of his life. The close relationship between his life and art has sometimes led people to overestimate the influence of the former on the latter. The constant portrayal of his family and himself was never done with autobiographical intent. His household was always available and in the same way as he habitually turned to his immediate surroundings for inspiration, he naturally used them as models. No other artist has ever laid bare his own life as intimately and extensively. Rubens, off-duty, made beautiful studies of his family, but for Rembrandt this distinction did not exist; his family was the starting point of his art.

His early self-portraits, e.g. H.1, (FIG. 12) were studies in a wide range of facial expression for which he took the model nearest at hand, namely himself. It was only later that his gaze became more searching and the practice grew into a form of self analysis. His life with Saskia, the birth of her children, and her final illness are recorded in moving detail in numerous drawings and etchings, although it is often only speculation which, for example, identifies a woman in bed as Saskia, since a portrait likeness was not the primary purpose of these studies, e.g. H. 53, (FIG. 16), *c.* 1635, and H. 54, *c.* 1638/9. *The Virgin and Child* (H. 17), *c.* 1635, with its air of domesticity, may well be a recollection of family life adapted to the subject in hand. After Saskia's death in 1642, there was a gap of about three years before Hendrickje Stoffels entered his household and took over Saskia's rôle in all but name. Like Saskia she was an ever available model and appears in many of his works. She may well be the subject of two of the finest drawings in the Museum. The first, *A girl sleeping* (H. 97) (FIG. 20), *c.* 1655/6, drawn entirely with the brush, is outstanding for the luminosity of the brush work, which, with a few suggestive strokes, succeeds in both indicating the form of the body and giving the scene depth and atmosphere. The other drawing which may depict her, *A girl seated* (H. 98a) (FIG. 22) must have been made about the same time and shows how he was able to impart the same luminous quality with the reed pen. The drawing is one of his most monumental works. His model is dressed up in Renaissance costume, a practice more common in his early years; in her left hand she appears to be holding a scroll of paper, while her right arm is not clearly delineated.

His son Titus was the other person who shared the artist's later years and played his part as a model. He is possibly the subject of three drawings, *A young man drawing* (H. 87), *A young man asleep* (H. 88) (FIG. 21) and *A young man resting his chin on his hand* (H. 85), all of which must have been drawn *c.* 1655, and show Rembrandt's vivid treatment with the reed pen.

In the 1650's Rembrandt made a series of large scale studies of the female nude. A pupil's drawing at Darmstadt shows Rembrandt seated amongst his pupils drawing from the model – a method of teaching which foreshadows the art school system – and it may well have been on such an occasion that he made the drawings in which he re-studied the female form. The outlines, simplified and bold, were drawn in pen and ink; wash was then added to build up the form or suggest background detail or atmosphere. Compared with his early essays in the nude these later studies have a classical grandeur and detachment; he was little concerned with describing texture and detail; the flesh is less material and simpler in outline: for instance, *A female nude standing by a chair* (H. 94), *A seated female nude bending forward* (H. 95), and *A seated female nude turned to the left with her arm supported by a sling* (H. 96) (FIG. 25), which was used as the basis of the etching, *Woman with an arrow* (Hind, *Etchings,* 303), dated 1661.

Rembrandt's drawings, particularly the later ones, have an air of finality which makes it apparent that his objective was clearly in his mind before he committed himself to paper. We do not find him feeling his way towards a solution, even though he sometimes re-worked a passage or made a false start as for example, can be seen on the *verso* of *An Oriental* (H. 64), where he drew a turbaned head, crossed it out and then turned the page. One might be tempted to conclude that he drew with great rapidity, but the little evidence there is, suggests that the reverse is true, and it is a mark of his genius that his significant generalizations of form give an overwhelming impression of spontaneity.

The drawings which show Rembrandt's powers of draughtsmanship at their most developed are those of religious, historical and mythological subjects. They are as complete works of art as paintings and etchings but, unlike most of these, are distinguished by their extreme brevity of execution. For the most part they were made with no further artistic intention in mind; they do not appear to have been collectors' pieces but were executed for the artist's own satisfaction, an approach which was a new concept of art in the seventeenth century. The artists of the sixteenth and seventeenth centuries generally used drawing as part of a working method. Drawings as finished works of art were not, however, unknown; Michelangelo's 'presentation drawings' immediately spring to mind or, nearer in date to Rembrandt, some drawings by Goltzius, but in each case the work is distinguished by its highly finished technique, equivalent to a painting. In Rembrandt's drawings on the other hand, there is a change of emphasis; his intention is not so much an exercise in style as the illustration of a particular theme. If he returns to the same theme in later years, it is to alter or enhance the psychological moment, and not to rework the composition in his latest manner. Following his career, one notices an increasing economy of line which has the effect of enhancing the impact of the subject itself. More and more he concentrates on the dramatic incident.

The Entombment of Christ (H. 2) (FIG. 1), dated 1630, is already masterly in composition and execution. There is nothing hesitant or stiff about the drawing; the red chalk flows from one figure to another; already he has developed a shorthand technique. The drawing originally represented the Raising of Lazarus, but Rembrandt changed his mind, shaded out the figure of Lazarus, and introduced the group round Christ being lowered into the tomb. The lines are, however, more numerous and diffuse than, for example, *Christ walking on the waves* (H. 72) (FIG. 2) which should be dated *c.* 1633 – Hind placed it about 1650 – where the composition emphasizes the story. He achieves his purpose with fewer, more descriptive lines. There is still an elaboration of detail in, for example, the figures of Christ and St Peter, though this contrasts with extreme simplicity in the drawing of the other two apostles. This flexibility is characteristic of the quill pen which Rembrandt favoured at this date. By the early 1640's he was arranging his figures in more closely knit groups as can be seen in *The Good Samaritan arriving at the inn* (H. 70) (FIG 3). The pen work here is more even throughout, particularly in the group round the body of the wounded traveller. The most striking quality about this drawing is the miraculous way in which the brown wash laid over the whole sheet in subtly varying shades of density suggests the atmosphere of night. In strong contrast to the extensive areas of brown wash are the few places where the artist has let the white of the paper show through in order to depict most tellingly the effect of brilliant localized light coming from three clearly defined sources: the windows of the inn, the candle lighting up the features of the innkeeper as he descends the steps, and, a supernatural light which floods the traveller's body and the figures around him. The natural colour of the paper which is usually treated as a neutral background has here become a positive element in the composition.

By the end of the 1640's Rembrandt was drawing in a simpler and more monumental style. In *Esau selling his birthright to Jacob* (H. 33) (FIG. 5), *c.* 1648/9, the outlines of the figures have gained in importance, though the hatching within these is still reminiscent of his earlier style. There is here a new concentration on the story itself, on the looks exchanged and the clasped hands sealing the bargain. *David and Absalom* (H. 90a) (FIG. 6), dating from *c.* 1655 or shortly afterwards, shows a similar scene limited to two protagonists. Brevity of execution and monumentality of conception are taken very much further. Hardly more than outline is described. The setting is limited to a massive column, which serves both to emphasize the figure of David and to set the scale of the sheet. The composition is very simple; the vertical accents of the figure of David and the column are balanced by the horizontal accent of the prostrate figure of Absalom. Everything draws attention to the psychological relationship of the two men. The figure of Absalom was redrawn so that, in the words of the Bible, 'he bowed himself *on his face to the ground* before the king'. The direction of David's gaze is emphasized by the angle at which he holds his staff, whilst the gesture of his left arm makes clear the deep emotion he feels. Even though Rembrandt depicts only one moment, the tragic implications of the whole story are present.

The British Museum possesses another version of *Christ walking on the waves* (H. 73) (FIG. 7), which must have been drawn at the end of the 1650's. Comparison with the version of twenty years earlier shows how far he had refined his art of illustration. The shift in the choice of the moment of the story is significant. St Peter is no longer struggling forward but has reached the support of Christ's arm. There is no strong effect of movement suddenly frozen. The figures are grouped more closely round Christ and St Peter, and only the oarsman does not contemplate the miraculous event. The lower viewpoint in this version brings the story more immediately to the spectator. The prow of the ship no longer breaks uncomfortably out of the composition but is so placed that it emphasizes the two main figures. The soft, broad lines of the reed pen, so unwieldy in describing detail, constitute the grandeur of his later style, and the painterly quality of the drawing shows Rembrandt moving towards an exclusive interest in painting. The *Scene from the life of Pyrrhus* (H. 97a) (FIG. 8), belongs to the same period and shows these characteristics to an even greater degree. The figures and the elephants are drawn in outline only in one thick stroke. Simplification could be carried no further and it foreshadows Rembrandt's last paintings where the paint was laid on with a palette knife.

Rembrandt's choice of subjects covers classical history and mythology, but by far the largest number are taken from the Bible. Earlier artists had of course used the Bible as a source, particularly the New Testament, but they tended to select the 'show pieces' which demanded elaborate pictorial treatment. Rembrandt, however, read it with new eyes and chose subjects which had never been represented before. His extensive knowledge, the result of constant reading, is revealed by the fact that it is sometimes difficult to identify the scene. A drawing (H. 39), *c.* 1644, in the British Museum, was catalogued by Hind as *The Flight into Egypt*, and was only later identified correctly as *The man of Gibeah offering hospitality to the Levite and his concubine*, an obscure incident from the Book of Judges (XIX, 17-20). Even today certain subjects remain disputed or unidentified. But an even more fundamental question of interpretation can arise. In a few cases it is difficult to decide whether a drawing is an illustration of a particular theme or only a genre study. An example is *An old man seated in a chair with an old woman standing beside him* (H. 58) (FIG. 4), *c.* 1642; it was catalogued by Hind as a genre study, but has since been interpreted as either Abraham and Sarah, or Jacob and Rachel listening to Joseph's account of his dreams; the latter is the more plausible identification – if indeed it is an illustration – and this was a favourite subject with Rembrandt although in every other example Joseph himself appears. This confusion shows how Rembrandt in order to give his Biblical subjects more immediacy, often depicted them in a contemporary setting.

In his selection of a theme Rembrandt shows a preference for a scene involving an intimate psychological relationship which meant that his compositions were often limited to few figures – the two versions, for example, of *Abraham thrusting out Hagar and Ishmael* (H. 34), *c.* 1640, and (H. 35) *c.* 1655. In both drawings the various emotions of each participant are clearly shown, whilst Sarah, hidden, watches the scene. Again in *Jacob asking the blessing of Isaac* (H. 37), *c.* 1655, Rembrandt treats the scene with great intimacy, adding a delightful touch of Sarah eavesdropping through the door. In all these drawings the spectator is so totally occupied in reading the story that the artist's means of depicting the scene never become obtrusive. It is this concentration on the subject which makes Rembrandt one of the most perfect illustrators, and it is ironical that with the exception of five etchings, his talents as an illustrator were completely ignored. The one fully illustrated Dutch Bible of the seventeenth century was the work of Jan Luyken, a mechanical and prolific draughtsman.

The landscape drawings make up the last category, though unfortunately their range is not fully represented in the British Museum. Landscape played a more limited rôle in Rembrandt's work and he did not turn to it until the middle of his life and had abandoned it before the end. It appears first in his drawings in the first half of the 1630's and was only later represented in painting and etching; after *c.* 1655 landscape as a subject in itself had largely disappeared. Though the span of his interest covers no more than about twenty years, he treated landscape with great thoroughness. Two distinct trends which run concurrently in his work can be seen in his approach, the romantic imaginary landscape and the realistic studies; but he reserved the former for painting whilst the latter was confined to his drawings and etchings. His walks around Amsterdam are recorded in numerous drawings and many of the places he depicted can be identified, e.g. *View from near the Anthoniespoort* (H. 114), and *The Amstel river near Kostverloren* (H. 108a) (FIG. 27). His early landscape style with its tendency to dwell on detail is hardly represented at all in the British Museum, though *The cottage on the banks of a river* (H. 99), sometimes doubted, is similar in conception to the landscape etchings of the early 1640's. Nearly all the British Museum drawings belong to the late 1640's and early 1650's and are drawn in the more classical and simplified style already described in connection with other subjects, e.g. *The Amstel river near Kostverloren* (H. 108a) (FIG. 27), dating from the early 1650's, depicts a motif which appears in several other drawings; the various features of the landscape, the trees and houses are defined in simple block-like shapes so that it is the volume of the landscape which impresses. On the other hand *A house amidst trees on the bank of a river* (H. 103) (FIG. 29), drawn about the same time or possibly a little earlier, shows the artist's ability to suggest shimmering light. The theme itself, a farm building surrounded by trees, is one of the most constant features of Dutch landscape, and was frequently depicted by Rembrandt. Sometimes it is the sculptural quality that the artist emphasizes, but here he is concerned with the effect of light seen through the trees and reflected from the water.

The flat landscape of Holland naturally offers two kinds of subject to the artist, either a distant panorama with a skyline of church spires, trees and sails, or a close-up view of, for example, farm buildings surrounded by trees: both types of subject are seen in Rembrandt's first landscape drawings and etchings. It was not until the 1650's, when the middle ground of the composition became the main focus of interest, that he succeeded in reconciling these two opposite kinds of motif, and gave his essays in landscape a measured and grander aspect.

In an age of romanticized popular history there is a tendency to revere the artists of the past who were neglected and ignored in their lifetime. Perhaps the two most popular heroes of the history of art are Rembrandt and Van Gogh who can never have been more admired than they are today, but were treated with incomprehension by many of their contemporaries. The romantic legend can, however, lay too much emphasis on the human side and in so doing often

D

tends to obscure the truth. That Rembrandt spent the latter part of his life in ever increasing poverty and that his work found little general appreciation is established fact, but it was undoubtedly he who made the first move in turning his back on the fashionable world. *The Night Watch* – the title itself is a misnomer – is often described as the turning point in the artist's career. The legend of his patrons' supposed dissatisfaction with the result of their commission has recently been unequivocally laid to rest, and the change in outlook which is evident in Rembrandt's works in the 1640's must be explained in other ways. When one considers that in not many years one of the most superficial artists of the age, Adriaen van der Werff, had become the fashionable painter in Holland and was to receive more adulation than any other Dutch artist of the seventeenth century, Rembrandt may well have felt he was only able to retain his artistic integrity by ignoring popular taste.

The personal interpretation of his art through his life is given a further fillip by the constant appearance of his family and himself in his works; the artist's mother, his wife Saskia, Hendrickje Stoffels, and his son, Titus, all appear before us in numerous guises, but it is above all the series of self-portraits depicting Rembrandt's increasingly introspective moods, that has encouraged this method of interpretation. This self-revelation goes hand in hand with the qualities of immediacy, psychological penetration and deep humanity which permeate all his works in every medium.

It is Rembrandt's drawings, above all, which appear so relevant today, and their modernity often makes it difficult to step back and see them in their historical context. Until the last years of his life when all his energies were devoted to painting, Rembrandt drew incessantly. But the historical significance of his drawings is not so much their sheer quantity – some 1,400 are known today – as the novel rôle they played in his art. For the Renaissance drawing was a means to an end; it became the method of working out ideas to receive their complete expression in painting, sculpture or architecture. The apotheosis of this approach was reached in the drawings of Rubens, the other great northern artist of the seventeenth century, nearly all of whose drawings can be directly connected with a painting or a project for a tapestry or piece of sculpture; very rarely does he appear to have made a drawing entirely for its own sake. In contrast, Rembrandt is the first artist to use drawing as a means of expression in its own right. Though he sometimes drew in preparation for a painting or an etching, by far the greater number of his drawings stand on their own as complete statements. With Rubens the sweep of creation carried him straight through from the first compositional sketch in pen and ink, the chalk study clarifying individual details, the oil sketch in colour, to the final work; the design was all important. Rembrandt, on the other hand, tended to develop each medium along certain lines of its own, confining his treatment of some subjects to one particular medium. There is a certain parallel with Henry Moore's statement of his own aims:

'Every material has its own individual qualities. It is only when the sculptor works direct, when there is an active relationship with his material, that the material can take its part in the shaping of an idea.'

SELECTED LITERATURE

GENERAL

H. DE GROOT *Die Urkunden über Rembrandt* (in German), The Hague, 1906. (All the documents relating to the artist)

A. M. HIND *Rembrandt*, London, 1932. (Series of general lectures)

J. ROSENBERG *Rembrandt*, 2 vols., Cambridge, Mass., 1948. (A general study of the artist and his work in all three media)

S. SLIVE *Rembrandt and his Critics, 1630-1730*, The Hague, 1953. (A study of criticism of the artist up to the time of Houbraken)

DRAWINGS

O. BENESCH *Rembrandt, Selected Drawings*, 2 vols., London, 1947. (A selection of drawings, with detailed notes and introduction)

O. BENESCH *Rembrandt, The Drawings of Rembrandt*, 6 vols., London, 1954-7.(A fully illustrated catalogue of all the drawings accepted as genuine by the author)

O. BENESCH *Rembrandt as a Draughtsman*, London, 1960. (A selection of drawings with notes of appreciation and a general introduction)

A. M. HIND *Catalogue of Drawings by Dutch and Flemish Artists in the British Museum*, vol. I, (*Rembrandt and his School*), London, 1915. (The official catalogue of the drawings in the British Museum)

F. LUGT *Mit Rembrandt in Amsterdam*, Amsterdam, 1915 (in Dutch) or Berlin, 1920 (in German). (Identifies the sites of many of the landscape drawings and etchings)

J. ROSENBERG *Great Draughtsmen*, London, 1960. (Chapter on Rembrandt's drawings – an essay of appreciation)

ETCHINGS

A. M. HIND *A Catalogue of Rembrandt's Etchings*, 2 vols., London, 1924. (second edition). (A complete catalogue arranged chronologically: fully illustrated)

L. MÜNZ *Rembrandt's Etchings*, 2 vols., London, 1952. (A complete catalogue, fully illustrated, arranged according to subject, with a technical introduction and a general survey of the artist's development in etching)

PAINTINGS

A. BREDIUS *The Paintings of Rembrandt*, London & New York (second edition *n.d*). (Illustrations of all the paintings; since 1945 there have been several selections of paintings published by the Phaidon Press)

ILLUSTRATIONS

1. THE ENTOMBMENT OF CHRIST (originally Raising of Lazarus). *1630.*
Red Chalk. 28 × 20.4 cm

2. CHRIST WALKING ON THE WAVES. c. 1633. Pen and brown ink. 16.8 × 26.5 cm

3. THE GOOD SAMARITAN ARRIVING AT THE INN. c. 1642. Pen and ink with brown wash, heightened with white. 18.4 × 28.7 cm

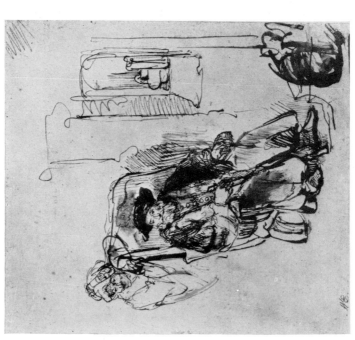

4. JACOB AND RACHEL LISTENING TO AN ACCOUNT OF
JOSEPH'S DREAMS (?). *c. 1642. Pen and ink with brown wash,
heightened with white. 18 × 16.3 cm*

5. ESAU SELLING HIS BIRTHRIGHT TO JACOB. *c. 1648/9.
Pen and ink with brown wash. 19.9 × 17.3 cm*

6. DAVID AND ABSALOM. *c. 1655. Reed pen and ink with brown wash, heightened with white. 16.5 × 21.6 cm*

7. CHRIST WALKING ON THE WAVES. *c. 1659. Reed pen and brown ink. 19 × 29 cm*

8. A SCENE FROM THE LIFE OF PYRRHUS. c. 1660. Reed pen and brown ink. 19.5 × 25 cm

9. COPY AFTER MANTEGNA'S 'CALUMNY OF APELLES'. *c. 1655. Pen and ink with brown wash. 26.3 × 43.2 cm*

10. COPY AFTER LEONARDO'S 'LAST SUPPER'. *c. 1635. Red chalk.*
12.4 × 20.9 cm

11. COPY AFTER A MOGUL MINIATURE (Four Dervishes).
c. 1656. Pen and ink with brown wash. 19.4 × 12.5 cm

13. CORNELIS CLAESZ ANSLO. *1640. Red chalk heightened with white.*
15.7 × 14.4 cm

12. SELF PORTRAIT. *c. 1628. Pen and brush and brown ink with*
grey wash. 12.6 × 9.5 cm

A NEGRO COMMANDER AND KETTLE DRUMMER.
*c. 1638. Pen and ink with brown wash, red chalk
and yellow water-colour, heightened
with white. 22.9 × 17 cm*

PUBLISHED BY
The Trustees of the British Museum
AND SOLD AT
The British Museum
AND BY
Bernard Quaritch Ltd, 11 Grafton Street, London w.1
Cambridge University Press, 200 Euston Road, London N.W.1
Kegan, Paul, Trench Trubner & Co. Ltd,
43 Great Russell Street, London w.c.1
Her Majesty's Stationery Office,
York House, Kingsway,
London w.c.2

Printed by
Eyre and Spottiswoode Limited
Her Majesty's Printers
at The Chiswick Press
London

THE
DRAWINGS OF
REMBRANDT

BY CHRISTOPHER
WHITE

*PUBLISHED
BY THE TRUSTEES OF
THE BRITISH MUSEUM
LONDON
1962*

18. TWO WOMEN TEACHING A CHILD TO WALK. *c. 1637. Red chalk. 10.4 × 12.9 cm*

19. A CHILD BEING TAUGHT TO WALK. *c. 1660. Reed pen and brown ink. 9.2 × 15.2 cm*

20. A GIRL SLEEPING (Hendrickje Stoffels?). *c. 1655. Brush drawing in brown ink.*
24.5 × 20.3 cm

21. A YOUNG MAN ASLEEP (Titus?). *c. 1655.*
Pen and ink with brown wash. 16.1 × 17.8 cm

22. A GIRL SEATED (Hendrickje Stoffels?). *c. 1655. Reed pen and brown ink.*
16.5 × 14.4 cm

23. DIANA AT THE BATH. *c. 1631. Black chalk with brown wash. 18.1 × 16.4 cm*

25. SEATED FEMALE NUDE. c. 1661. Pen and
brown ink with brown and grey wash, heightened with
white. 29.8 × 18.3 cm

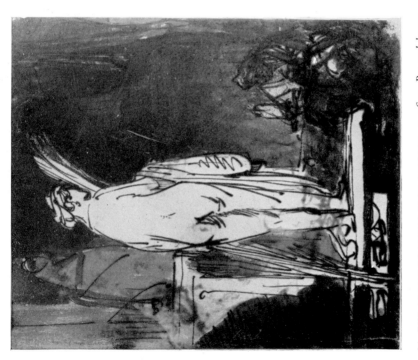

24. THE ARTIST DRAWING FROM A MODEL. c. 1639. Pen and brown
ink with brown wash. 18.7 × 16.2 cm

49

26. AN ELEPHANT. c. 1637. Black chalk. 17.7 × 25.5 cm

27. THE AMSTEL RIVER NEAR KOSTVERLOREN. *c. 1653. Reed pen and brown ink.*
12.6 × 19.7 cm

28. A CHAINED LIONESS. *c. 1641. Black chalk with grey wash, heightened with white*
12.6 × 18.1 cm

51

29. HOUSE AMIDST TREES. c. 1650. Pen and black ink with grey wash. 15·6 × 23·3 cm

52